'If you're looking for an accessible, energetic and fun
emotional side of climate change, look no further. Th
readers on as it teaches them how to harness eco-em
purposeful and personally sustainable climate action. It rightfully points out
the bright side of the challenge we all face.'

– Britt Wray, PhD, author of Generation Dread and Planetary
Health Fellow, Stanford University School of Medicine

'I wish we'd all read this when we were kids, perhaps we would already be
living all the climate solutions.'

– Arizona Muse, supermodel, parent and sustainability activist

'The perfect toolkit for families affected by eco-anxiety. It contains engaging
facts, great practical ideas and through carefully chosen keywords, it
manages to concisely unravel tricky sustainability issues. It also clearly
explains the importance of self-care for eco-warriors.'

– Mireille Digard, educator and Climate Reality Leader

'You Are Unstoppable! is a gift to young people – and to the parents, teachers
and caregivers who love them. Climate change can be an overwhelming
topic, but this book navigates the difficult terrain of climate emotions with
clarity, compassion and honesty. Filled with ideas that are both practical and
empowering, You Are Unstoppable! will help young people learn how to care for
themselves and each other while caring for the planet. As a parent, I'm deeply
grateful this book exists.'

– Elizabeth Bechard, Moms Clean Air Force and author
of Parenting in a Changing Climate

'Thank you so much for finally making the book I needed in my youth!'

– Daze Aghaji, climate justice activist

'Grounded in evidence-based hope and realistic steps for the average student
of the Earth! As a young person, I think this is a must-read for every student
struggling to understand the climate crisis. It's not easy to talk about it or
learn about it. But with this book, I felt like I can relate and have sustainable
steps to take to help protect the planet! Building a sustainable future requires
thousands of us to understand a complex problem but recognize the solutions
have always existed! This book offers the promise of working together to build
a climate-positive world that connects science, culture and hope!'

– Isaias Hernandez, environmental educator, climate justice
activist and creator of @QueerBrownVegan

'Such an important book to alleviate climate anxiety and harness change.'

– Anya Hindmarch, sustainable fashion designer and author

of related interest

You Can Make a Difference!
A Creative Workbook and Journal for Young Activists
Sherry Paris
ISBN 978 1 78775 648 9
eISBN 978 1 78775 649 6

You Can Change the World!
Everyday Teen Heroes Making a Difference Everywhere
Margaret Rooke
Forewords by Taylor Richardson and Katie Hodgetts @KTclimate
Illustrated by Kara McHale
ISBN 978 1 78592 502 3
eISBN 978 1 78450 897 5

Something Bad Happened
A Kid's Guide to Coping With Events in the News
Dr Dawn Huebner
Illustrated by Kara McHale
ISBN 978 1 78775 074 6
eISBN 978 1 78775 075 3

You Are Unstoppable!

How to Understand Your Feelings about Climate Change and Take Positive Action Together

Megan Kennedy-Woodard and Dr Patrick Kennedy-Williams

Illustrated by Jordanna George

Jessica Kingsley Publishers

London and Philadelphia

First published in Great Britain in 2023 by Jessica Kingsley Publishers
An imprint of John Murray Press

1

Front cover image source: Jordanna George.

A CIP catalogue record for this title is available from the British Library and the Library of Congress

ISBN 978 1 83997 422 9
eISBN 978 1 83997 423 6

Printed and bound in Great Britain by Clays Limited

Jessica Kingsley Publishers' policy is to use papers that are natural, renewable and recyclable products and made from wood grown in sustainable forests. The cover is printed on uncoated board to eliminate the use of plastic in the manufacturing of this book. The logging and manufacturing processes are expected to conform to the environmental regulations of the country of origin.

Jessica Kingsley Publishers
Carmelite House
50 Victoria Embankment
London EC4Y 0DZ

www.jkp.com

John Murray Press
Part of Hodder & Stoughton Limited
An Hachette UK Company

To Wyatt and Arizona. You are as brave, wild, smart and funny as you are kind. We adore you.

To our families and friends.

To young people from around the world, we hear you and we see you.

To our beautiful, improbable planet.

Special thanks to Claudia Van Luchene's English ~~accent~~ grammar, and the science wisdom of Professor Mark Maslin and Dr Louise Dalton.

Finally, we are so grateful to the inspirational contributors of this book. Thank you for sharing your stories, your openness and your activism.

Contents

'When it comes to activism, I felt that the way to deal with those difficult emotions was to cling to optimism, determination and hope.'

Clover Hogan, youth activist and
founder of Force of Nature

It's Nice to Meet You

Hey! We are climate psychologists.

I'm Megan, and I'm a coaching psychologist. I love the beach, cooking and animals.

I'm Patrick, and I'm a clinical psychologist. I love the mountains, music and cycling.

We've got two wild and curious children...and lots of pets!

As a family who loves our planet, we were all finding it really emotional and difficult to learn about **CLIMATE CHANGE**. That's why it feels so important for us to take **CLIMATE ACTION**. Since we were already psychologists and interested in how people's minds work, we threw ourselves into understanding **CLIMATE PSYCHOLOGY**.

In other words, we wanted to understand how our minds react when we think about, hear about, or experience climate change. Now we help people (like you!) learn to turn their feelings about climate change – like worry, **ANXIETY**, sadness or anger – into climate action that will help them AND the planet.

This book will help you to:

- notice feelings that come up when you think or hear about climate change, and know what to do about them
- support yourself by becoming a champion of self-care
- turn **climate anxiety** into sustainable **climate action**
- talk to people about climate change and inspire others
- enjoy the climate work you do!

How to Use This Book

**It's not like flicking a switch – although
turning off the lights saves energy!**

Changing our mindset and our behaviour takes time. You
don't have to read this whole book in one go. And you don't
have to do climate work perfectly, either! If you have a
friend or family member who is also experiencing big
climate emotions (which we sometimes also call **ECO-
EMOTIONS**), why not read through and do the work
together? Take it step by step and chapter by chapter.

Climate journaling – the power of writing it down

Have you ever seen a pot on a stove bubble over? That's
what our brains do sometimes: they bubble over with
thoughts and emotions. A great way to turn down that
mental heat is to pour out some of what is in the pot.
We can do this by writing down how we feel.

Throughout this book we will ask you some BIG
QUESTIONS. Try to really think about what they

mean and how they feel for you. Yes, you! Because you matter, and your feelings and actions matter. It's a great idea to have a climate journal where all your climate emotions, thoughts, ideas and goals can collect in one place. This will be a great tool to organize your plans to help the planet.

You can use this journal as you work your way through this book, but you can also reach for it ANY TIME to write down how you feel, or any new ideas you might have! You might also want to show it to others so they know how you are feeling and what you are working on.

Making your climate journal

Remember: we are being eco-friendly here, people! You don't need to run to the store and buy a new notebook. You might have an old one lying around that has a few scribbles but lots of empty pages. Or perhaps you could make one using recycled materials and scraps of paper from around the house. Get creative.

Eco-warriors like you!

There are lots of quotes throughout the book from other young people around the world who have experienced lots of emotions after hearing about or experiencing climate change. These unstoppable young people are taking action to help the planet, and they shared these stories with us (and you!) when we were writing this book. We hope you find their stories inspiring.

Your first climate action: Get the grown-ups involved

Throughout this book, you will learn how important it is to talk about climate change and also how important it is to ask for support! This is your first opportunity to practise both. Ready?

You see, the adults have a role to play too. Sometimes adults have been criticized for not acting quickly enough to help the planet. But we know that so many adults are ready and willing to help you young people to change the world. Your 'adult **ALLIES**' are on hand to help you.

Hand this book to your parent or guardian and tell them it would mean the world to you if they read the last chapter, 'For Adults and Educators'. Go on, put them to work!

Allies are people who are on our team. They often believe in the same causes, and are in a good position to help us achieve our aims. We can also be allies for others.

Chapter 1

New Bee-Haviour

> All this pollution doesn't make me feel good, so at home we do a lot of things like composting and recycling. I don't like wasting. My dad had an idea. We made a bug hotel. We used old recycled wood and pine cones and bamboo and flowers. We were painting it all together and we were all happy and smiley and laughing. We didn't buy anything for it, just used what we had; now it's a home for lots of animals. It was so fun, and we like going and seeing what might be in there.
>
> Camilla, France

Think about the change you could ignite by championing our most valuable **ASSET**: the planet!

Wait, we take that back! The planet is not an asset...and that is part of the problem. We usually think about the Earth as something we take things from, and this has to change. We need to think of ourselves and the Earth as partners. We need to give more and take less. This starts with each and every one of us. As we learn to care for the Earth and take climate action, we become one small (but important) part of the solution.

Consider this African proverb, quoted by the Dalai Lama: 'If you think you are too small to make a difference, try sleeping with a mosquito.' That one little thing will make a big difference to you when you wake up, covered in itchy bites. But what if there were millions of mosquitos? You'd certainly know it in the morning!

It's helpful to think about climate action in this way too. Yes, one person can make a small difference, but guess what? There are millions of people taking millions of positive actions, and this can make a BIG difference. In a recent survey in England, over 80% of young people (aged between 8 and 15) said that they want to take action to help the planet.[1] That's around 5.5 MILLION young people in England alone![2]

Let's be more like the honeybees!

The problem is, for a long time, humans have been treating the planet a lot like mosquitos treat us – we've been taking something away and causing harm.[3]

Let's talk about **SYMBIOSIS**.

> **Symbiosis** is a relationship that is cooperative, where two (or more) different things get along together and help each other out.

So instead of something that takes away or extracts, like mosquitos, let's think about something that cooperates... like bees. Although some species of bee are solitary (meaning they live alone), many species (like our sweet friend, the honeybee) are social. This means they live together and support each other. But it doesn't end there.

Honeybees have a symbiotic relationship with flowering plants, because the flowers provide nectar to feed the bees, and in return, the bees carry pollen from one plant to the next, which helps the plant species to reproduce.

 The extra wonderful thing for you and me (besides the delicious honey, of course) is that bees also help pollinate loads of different fruit and vegetable species (like oranges, blueberries, apples, peaches, tomatoes and cucumbers), meaning that we depend on these little guys too. With each single effort from millions of bees, think of all the species that are supported, and all the food that is produced because of their cooperation with each other and with their environment.

Bees set a great example of how to be an ally to the planet. Did you know these cool facts about these buzzy-fuzzy folks? We have a lot in common with them![4]

   Honeybees probably don't want to sting you because if they do, well, they'll die.

Just like a bee stinging someone, if we hurt the planet, we hurt ourselves. The more pain we cause the Earth, the more it hurts other humans, other species and the rest of the natural world. Everything we do has an effect on our planet...but this is good news, because our positive actions have positive effects!

   Honeybees are constantly working together – every bee has a role to play.

Bee colonies help one other by caring for the sick, sharing food, even keeping each other at the perfect temperature (not too warm, not too cold). Just like the buzzy bees, every human has a role to play too. Whoever we are, it's important that we pay attention to and learn about the experiences of people different to ourselves and become each other's allies.

 Can you believe that there are over 20,000 different species of bees that can be found on all the continents, except Antarctica?

There are so many of us humans and we are all so different, but we also have so many interests and goals in common. Across the globe, there are people who are just like you, who are doing essential climate work. We may be doing it in different ways and under different circumstances, but we are all invested in the future and connected to our ecosystems (even in Antarctica)!

 In order to make just a kilogram of honey, bees basically do the same as flying around the world three times.

Helping our planet takes a lot of work, and this can sometimes feel really hard. That's okay! Even the busiest bee knows it's important to stop and smell the flowers. When we take time to rest and rejuvenate, we're taking care of ourselves and making sure we can keep going with our climate work.

 Nearly 75% of our main crops around the world and 90% of wild plants depend on pollination from animals. That means that out of three bites of your food, one is probably thanks to a pollinator.

Wow, that sounds exhausting! Luckily, there are lots of ways we can help our bee friends just like they help us. Try lending a hand to a struggling bee by putting it on a flower or giving it sugar water. Ask your friends and family not to kill bees or damage their hives. Planting bee-friendly flowers and trees in your garden or even in a window box can make a difference in keeping bees busy, us fed and our ecosystems healthy.

Remember this: our ideas and habits can inspire climate positive bee-haviour in others. Before we know it, the world will be a better place!

There are lots of ideas throughout this book to help you be more bee! Look out for the friendly bee icon:

 Remember Camilla (from the start of this chapter)? You could make a bug hotel just like she did. Here are some instructions on how to do it.

How to build a bug hotel

The great thing about bug hotels is that you can use all kinds of materials that you can collect in nature or probably already have. Here are the instructions for you (and a trusted adult) to follow:

1. Start by stacking old pallets and bricks with space in between. These are great for the main structure of your hotel.
2. Then fill the spaces with drilled logs, bamboo or hollowed sticks. Use old, small pots filled with moss, rocks, dried leaves, pine cones, sand, soil, straw, and anything else you think a creepy crawly would enjoy. You can build these up to a metre high (making sure the base is secure), or keep it closer to the ground.
3. Roof time – old tiles or planks on top help keep your bug hotel dry.
4. Finally, encourage your bug guests to visit by spreading wildflower seeds around your bug hotel.

Chapter 2

What Is Climate Change?

Let's ask our good friend, the brilliant climate scientist, Professor Mark Maslin, what exactly climate change is.

Mark loves environmental science and has written some awesome books, including *Climate Change: A Very Short Introduction*,[1] and one of our favourites, *How to Save our Planet: The Facts*.[2] He gives lots of inspiring talks and isn't at all bad at football! Here's what he has to say about climate change:

> Climate change is one of the major challenges facing us all this century. Climate change will continue to increase the temperature of the Earth and raise sea level around the world. We are already seeing more extreme weather events such as droughts, heat waves (when the weather gets really hot), wildfires, floods, and storms. It threatens the health and way of life for billions of people.
>
> Harmful greenhouse gases, like methane and carbon dioxide, things that humans are producing too much of, by the way we farm, our transportation, how we make things and more, are being pumped into our atmosphere and dangerously heating up our planet.

Yeesh, did that seem overwhelming and scary? It's important for us all to understand the science behind climate change, but do 'check in' with yourself when you're reading about it.

'Checking in' means taking a moment to notice how you are feeling and what thoughts you are having. A handy tip to help you work out the difference between feelings (also called 'emotions') and thoughts is that you can usually describe a feeling or emotion in one word (like 'happy', 'proud' or 'nervous') whereas thoughts can be described using a sentence (like 'Wow, climate change sounds really bad' or 'What can I do to help?').

Grab your climate journal!

This book encourages you to check in with yourself when you hear about climate change. We want to actively notice our emotions and understand that what we are feeling is okay. We will learn how to manage these feelings and support ourselves, so if reading that just made you feel wobbly, this is a helpful sign that you care. So, having just read Mark's explanation of climate change, how are you feeling? What thoughts are popping into your mind? Get journaling.

Where is climate change happening?

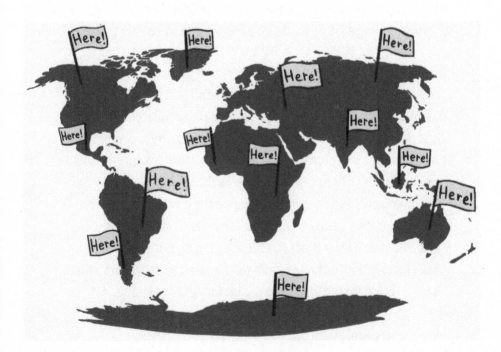

The bad news: climate change is everywhere. The more we see it, the more it can make us feel strong climate emotions. The good news: the solutions to climate change are everywhere as well, and so are the scientists, activists and people of all generations who are working hard to reverse global warming!

US Vice President and climate activist Al Gore once said, 'I believe the sustainability revolution is unstoppable',[3] and we agree! We think you, and the millions around the world who care about this planet, are unstoppable.

Who is affected by climate change?

It's really important to recognize that many people all over the world are already being affected by climate change...and a lot of the people most affected by climate change have done the least to add to the problem:

I met with an Indigenous leader of our land and he talked to us about how they were being harassed and displaced...all for just protecting the planet, and their homeland. He just ever so simply said, as he chuckled and shrugged, 'That is why we have no choice but to fight back.' And it was the simplicity of how he said it...even with positivity, despite the awful things he is experiencing – he wasn't trying to convince us or anything, he just said it as a matter of fact. I started crying and just realized – he's right. This is it. I have to join the fight of the people who have been fighting for the life of the planet for decades.

Mitzi Jonelle Tan, youth activist, organizer
for Fridays For Future, Philippines

Most Affected People and Areas (MAPA)

MAPA means 'Most Affected People and Areas'. People living in these areas around the world are dealing with the worst of climate change right now, and they are at the highest risk in the future (MAPA areas include much of the **GLOBAL SOUTH**). For a long time, governments have ignored their warnings. Folks have lost loved ones, their land and their ways of life. They may be punished for protesting and asking for **CLIMATE JUSTICE** and safety.

There are so many incredible activists in these areas who are already on the front lines of the climate crisis battlefield. It is so important that we listen to what they are going through and what they want to change. We need to put pressure on the adults in charge (particularly governments and large companies) to listen to the voices from MAPA.

> **Climate justice** means that the climate crisis is not just about defending the environment, but also fighting for the rights of all the people around the world who are treated unfairly (often when they are trying to take important climate action).

As well as MAPA **regions** (areas around the world), there are also **groups** of people who belong to MAPA. Many of these groups have been ignored when it comes to the impact that climate change has already had on them (and will have on them in the future).

For example, women, people from BIPOC (Black, Indigenous and people of colour) and LGBTQ+ (Lesbian, Gay, Bisexual, Transgender, Queer or Questioning) communities, people in poorer areas and people who are differently abled are often **MARGINALIZED**, which means they are at greater risk from extreme weather events and **SOCIAL INJUSTICES**.

They may also be overlooked for all the hard work they do to protect and heal our planet. Climate action is intersectional, which means that we need to consider the social injustices of our climate allies around the world and fight for their rights as well.[4]

Marginalized means being made deliberately less powerful or influential.

Social injustices are ways in which people from different communities or backgrounds are treated unfairly, or they have access to fewer opportunities in life.

Why don't people care?!

So now we know that climate change is harming our planet and that we have to cut greenhouse gas emissions to stop climate change. Science proves it, and scientists have been going bonkers trying to get people to listen to the facts! So why don't some people seem to care? Why aren't we all doing everything we can to stop this?

The first thing to say is that sometimes it might FEEL like nobody cares, but actually, more and more people are finally listening. Climate change is now being seen as an emergency around the world, and most people agree that it is the most important challenge facing humanity.

However, everybody isn't on board quite yet. Some people don't want to listen for a lot of reasons. Often, we can't see climate change happening because it can be invisible or feel far away, like it won't change our lives.

Who cares about cows farting (which releases harmful methane) or the temperature rising by 1.5 degrees? It can be hard for some people to understand these as real, important threats because they don't look like, for example, a tiger about to pounce on us. This is confusing for the part of our brain that looks for danger. Climate change is a sneaky villain, and that's why it's hard for some people to care.

It's also important to understand that there have been people and organizations that DON'T want us to know the truth. The fossil fuels industries (that produce coal, oil and natural gas) have been trying to tell us that climate change isn't a very serious problem.

They have also tried putting the blame on individual people and families, making it seem like it's all our fault and down to us to solve. Sometimes they even pretend to want to be part of the solution. This is called **GREENWASHING**.

They want to delay action and have done lots of sneaky things themselves to avoid the move towards renewable energy (meaning to create electricity from wind, the sun or even the ocean tides). They have deliberately caused confusion and doubt. Many people feel very angry about this, and that is okay. It's wrong that they have done this.

> **Greenwashing** is when groups (usually businesses or governments) try to convince everybody that they are taking action to help the planet, when, in fact, they are not.

Climate change can also be something that people don't want to think about (or don't want to believe is a real problem) because it feels uncomfortable or scary. Humans are creatures of habit and like to avoid discomfort and inconvenience. To help fight climate change, someone might have to try something new, or stop doing something they are familiar with, or that is part of their daily routine.

This is difficult because people don't really like being told what to do, and change can feel hard. If we tell people who love cheeseburgers to go vegan, they probably won't be happy about it. We like the comfort of what we know, even if it's more dangerous in the long run. It's really important to be talking about climate change, how it makes us feel and what we are doing about it, because this can INSPIRE others rather than making them feel defensive.

This past year I worked on creating a film with a peer on climate anxiety. We had interviewed a variety of activists who specialize in this area to bring in different perspectives. This journey has given me further knowledge about this issue and now I'm ready to take steps to help others. In addition, I've been working on a film with a director in the UK. In this film, I reflect on my experiences of climate change in my family's hometown, Delhi and an activist talks about the issue in my state, Virginia.
I believe it is crucial to talk about climate change at school because passion and change will spark within young minds to tackle this issue with great impact.

Aarushi, USA

The truth is that LOTS of people care!

This isn't a book about climate change; this is a book about how climate change makes us feel and what we can do about it. But when we discuss climate change with those around us, we do want to know what we're talking about!

We love scientists because they spend their time doing research to understand climate change. They can then, in turn, help us to understand what's happening to our planet and how we can help.

Unfortunately, there is also a lot of information out there that can be puzzling; remember, some people even *try* to make climate information confusing, so people don't understand what is happening and what they need to do to help. That's why it's essential that we spread truthful information when we discuss this topic!

The great news is that if we communicate in clever and inspiring ways, we can get people thinking about the world in a different way. You may get one person thinking about just one small shift they could make in their lives...then, from that change, they might feel inspired to make more changes! They will tell their friends about what they're doing differently, and their friends will tell their friends! This is a simple but very effective way to spread change.

Megan's lovely dad David didn't know much about electric cars. Megan started talking to him about how great her electric car is, which inspired him. When it was time for him to get a new car, he got an electric one! But it didn't stop there... Patrick told him about how great their composting was for their garden (and the planet, because composting food waste above ground stops it releasing harmful methane if it goes into landfill). Now guess who is composting, using solar energy and telling his friends about how great it is? That's right, David!

By focusing on the positivity of our actions, we're sending a message out that change doesn't have to be difficult or unpleasant; it can actually be interesting, fun, inspiring and contagious. Who could you talk to about how cool all your climate action is? Have conversations with lots of people from all walks of life.

Keep buzzing in their ear and they will eventually see how sweet this work can bee!

Chapter 3

Young People Just Like You

Remember Professor Mark Maslin from Chapter 2? He knows that young people are leading the movement to stop climate change in its tracks. It's the adults who need to catch up. As well as explaining what climate change is, Mark is full of helpful advice on what we can all be doing:

We need governments and businesses to take responsibility, to stop arguing and thinking about how to make money and get more power. We need to all be thinking about what we can do and what kind of society we want to live in, but also what kind of relationship we want to have with our planet. Only by working together can we deal with one of the greatest crises that has ever faced humanity.

We have the technology, the resources, the experts and the money to deal with climate change. What we need is for the adults to wake up! We need the politicians to take action and change laws so that we can have the win-win solutions needed to make a better, safer, healthier and hopefully happier world. Young people are at the heart of understanding our huge environmental crisis. School strikes and protests are increasing public pressure for real change.

New laws and ways of thinking are starting to emerge. We just need to do all these great things quicker! But together we can all change the world for the better.

Thanks, Mark!

You didn't start the fire

As a young person, you are far more likely to be aware of the dangers of climate change. You learn about it in school. You hear about it on the news and radio, and you might see pictures and videos about climate change on the internet and social media. You may look around and see plastic waste, cars spewing pollution, and politicians not doing nearly enough.

More and more, adults are realizing that it is the younger people who 'get it'. You folks didn't make this mess. You didn't start the fire, but now you're being asked to put it out. This might not seem fair. You may feel scared, sad, angry or hopeless.

It's okay to feel like this!

Young people ALL OVER THE WORLD experience these feelings. And these frightening events can not only hurt the planet, but they can be hard on your mental health and your ability to fight climate change as well. It's important to remember that these are totally normal emotional responses and there is nothing wrong with how you're feeling.

We want to make climate action feel enjoyable and easy. Some of the most amazing climate activists in the world say that their work makes them feel stronger. They say that they feel more connected to the world around them, that they feel inspired, and that they love their work. Pretty cool, right? When we break this work into easy, manageable steps, we turn big emotions into big actions.

Chapter 4

Understanding Our Eco-Emotions

They talked about climate anxiety in a magazine we read. It can be quite depressing. My mum gets a bit down about it, but I am not feeling it too much right now because when we do the strikes, I know that there are other people that feel the same way. We like being with people who are doing climate stuff too.

Sometimes it can feel kind of depressing when you hear things that are so bad, and how it's gonna be really bad in the future and we are causing it, but then later you'll hear about someone who has invented new technology that's helping so much. Emotionally it's a bit of a road, up and down, up and down.

Ben, UK

Meet Mr Climate Anxiety (also known as Mr Eco-Anxiety)

Climate anxiety can be felt by anyone of any age, anywhere in the world. Studies show that younger people are feeling more and more worried about the climate and the future, as well as anger towards adults (particularly companies and governments) for not doing enough. Those who live in areas that are more affected by climate change often feel more climate anxiety (in areas that have experienced extreme weather, like flooding or wildfires, for example).

When climate anxiety gets too big, it makes us feel like we can't enjoy our lives. We may pull away from the people we love, and it may be harder to study or sleep at night. We might find it really hard to stop worries about the troubles of the planet. Although it's called climate **anxiety** (which means feeling scared, panicked or worried), you might also feel grief, sadness and anger. So it makes more sense to call them **eco-emotions** (or climate emotions).

I am so grateful for my friends; having friends who know. You don't have to explain it. They know. And it's funny in this online world – we will just call each other and be quiet together. And these are friends that are across the globe. My best friends are from India and the Netherlands and we've never met. We only see the top half of each other's bodies on Zoom but there is this connection because we understand this climate pain and grief.

Mitzi Jonelle Tan, youth activist, organizer
for Fridays For Future, Philippines

Emotions are very important!

Trying to force our eco-emotions away is a bit like trying to hold a big beach ball underwater for a long time: it's really hard! The longer we push our eco-emotions down, the harder they will eventually pop up and whack us in the face. Holding that emotional beach ball underwater is exhausting and something we won't be able to do for very long. This may mean that we give up on our climate action, or never feel like what we're doing is enough.

We can learn a lot from what these emotions are trying to tell us. We can let these feelings help us and motivate us.

We can use them as a signal that we have something difficult to do...and we are totally capable of doing difficult things! When we notice and name our emotions, which we will practise, we can connect with what we care about. We can stand up to the discomfort because we know we are strong enough and good enough and that our efforts matter. We can do ALL the hard things necessary to fight climate change!

The truth is, a little anxiety can be helpful because it pushes us into action. But when our climate anxiety takes over, it makes it much harder for us to do what we need to do to make a difference. Before the worry gets to be too much, we need to help ourselves so that we can keep helping the planet.

> When I see people polluting it makes me feel sad and it makes me think of that saying, '123, there is no Planet B' and I worry that the planet is heating up. If this planet didn't have life on it, it would look like a moon. No plants, no animals, no life.
>
> Wyatt, France

Noticing our emotions

Let's do a thought experiment. It's not meant to make us feel great, but it will help in the long run (we promise!).

Is there a time you remember when you felt really scared or angry about climate change? Remember the section of this book where Mark Maslin explained some climate facts to us? Think of seeing plastic in our seas, wildfires and flooding. We see people and governments doing nothing. We see species under threat, people littering, dangerous hurricanes, starving polar bears...there is so much that needs to be done.

Now, close your eyes and think really hard about these problems for 30 seconds. After you're done, open your eyes.

How did that experiment make you FEEL?

What THOUGHTS were you thinking?

Were there any SENSATIONS in your body, like butterflies in your stomach, or your heart pumping faster?

Grab your journal and note down the thoughts, feelings and sensations that came up for you.

When I hear difficult climate news, I think the feeling of overwhelm is something that's strongest with me. It's a very out of body experience. I get the feeling that I am not in my body any more. I see myself from a different angle, which is strange and it feels like being seasick but not moving at the same time. I feel like I am feeling too much all at once. I use some grounding exercises, like visualizing roots growing from my feet into the ground or using mantras that remind me 'I am doing the work that I need to do to make sure that the nature I love is protected'.

Daze, youth climate activist, UK

If you were feeling strong eco-emotions, don't worry. It's normal. Your mind and body are reacting to threatening information, and that is exactly what they are meant to do! In fact, we can thank our body and mind for responding this way. It has helped humans avoid danger for thousands of years.

We know that thought experiment wasn't fun, but it does help us notice how our body and mind respond to difficult information about the climate. When we observe our reactions, we can discover some of the **TRIGGERS** (more on these soon) that cause difficult feelings about climate change. By carefully noticing our thoughts and our body's responses to climate information, we can build a plan to support ourselves when we're feeling big eco-emotions.

But what precisely is happening in our brain when we feel strong emotions like anxiety anyway?

The fight, flight or freeze system

The fight, flight or freeze system is an incredible safety feature of our brains. In fact, it is found across the whole animal kingdom. It is an automatic response that our brain goes into when we feel like we are under threat. This is awesome when we need to punch through a window to escape a fire (fight), run away or dodge something coming towards us (flight), or hold perfectly still if a wasp is near (freeze). Our fight, flight or freeze system can keep us safe.

The problem is that modern life makes this response more complicated. These modern-day threats are sometimes slightly different, so our body's response doesn't always feel quite so helpful. For example, if we are talking in front of a big group of people, we might feel scared and freeze, even though we are not actually in any danger. Or we might run away from a new challenge because we've never tried it before.

The fight, flight or freeze system isn't anyone's fault. We just have it. It also isn't dangerous to us; it won't do us any harm. However, when it's 'switched on' (a process called sympathetic nervous system activation), your brain prepares your whole body to react to danger. It does this by releasing hormones like adrenaline and cortisol that make us feel super-aware and in high alert mode.

This may feel a little uncomfortable in your body. You probably recognize the fight, flight or freeze system being switched on as the feeling of 'anxiety' or 'anger'.

Here are some physical signs that your fight, flight or freeze system might be switched on:

- fast heartbeat
- sweaty palms
- tightness in your throat
- feeling panicked
- butterflies in your stomach, or feeling sick
- tingling in your fingers or toes
- feeling like you need to go to the toilet.

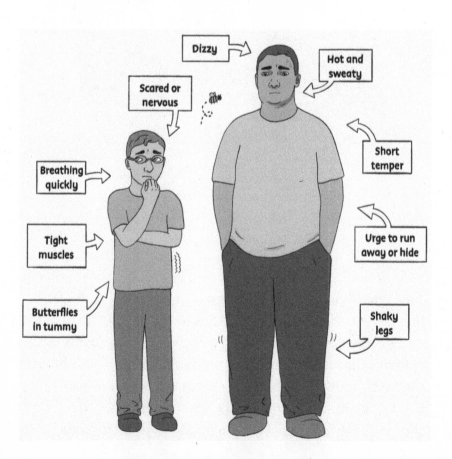

When I think about global warming I feel stressed and that it's gross and annoying. I know some people think it's nothing and it's those people that seem to pollute the most. When I feel that, my senses feel wonky and blocked – I feel like I can only hear or see the person who is polluting.

Arizona, USA

Let's break out our climate journals once again!

Draw a picture of yourself in your journal and label it with what you feel and where you feel it when you receive information about the climate crisis. Noticing your physical reactions will give you clues that you are having a response to information about the climate, and just knowing this can help us accept these feelings and be kinder to ourselves. This can also help us 'override' these feelings when they are too strong. We can remind ourselves, 'This is our fight, flight or freeze system'.

'Buzz through the fight, flight or freeze system'

The good news is that you can also learn to switch off your fight, flight or freeze system. In fact, our bodies have an amazing way of calming down, which we call the parasympathetic nervous system (or 'rest and digest'). Once our brain has decided that the threat has passed, it returns the body to its normal state. Our heart rate slows down, and so does our breathing. These help restore balance to our minds and bodies, and we feel calmer again. However, because threats like climate change don't just 'go away' overnight, it's important to find ways to help our bodies into 'rest and digest'.

We can do this by 'breathing like a bee'!

Breathe like a bee!

Start by closing your eyes and taking a slow, deep 'belly breath'. Breathe in through your nose for five seconds and see if you can feel your belly inflating like a balloon. Then breathe out slowly through your mouth, feeling the belly balloon lowering as you do so. But then, as you breathe out, make a bzzzzzzzzz noise, just like a bee. See how long you can breathe out for. Make the bee breath as long as you can! Get someone around you to join you. You can say, 'I am feeling a little anxious. Would you try something with me?' It might feel a little silly at first, but actually, a bit of humour can help relax us.

By doing this even for one minute, you can trigger your 'rest and digest' system and switch off the fight, flight or freeze system.

Are you in the Scarcity Zone (booooo) or the Abundance Zone (WOOHOO)?

Think of these each as a separate mental space.

The word **SCARCITY** looks a bit like the word 'SCARY' for a reason...it means feeling like there isn't enough. When we talk about scarcity with climate change, we think things like:

Whatever I do won't matter, it won't be enough.

There isn't enough time.

I haven't been good enough.

When we're thinking about our climate work from inside the Scarcity Zone, it can be really hard for us to notice all the action we are taking and how much we can still do. It feels hard to feel proud, motivated or committed...not a great space to be in.

ABUNDANCE means that there's a lot of something. See the 'DANCE' part of the word ABUNDANCE. We can remember that this is the place where we feel like we are 'in the flow' and on the right track, doing things that feel good for us. When we're in the Abundance Zone, this means that we do our climate work from a place where we feel that our actions are important, that we can make a difference, and that we can influence other people. We think thoughts like:

I've got this!

We are making such a great change.

Look how many of us there are taking climate action.

This is awesome!

Positive self-talk (aka 'mantras') and reminding ourselves of times we have achieved a goal can all help to return our minds to the Abundance Zone. When you feel like you are in the Abundance Zone, take some time to write down some of your successes and phrases (mantras) that you can repeat to yourself later, when you need them.

Chapter 5

Getting Out of Your Head

Remember: when we have a lot of thoughts and feelings floating around in our mind, it can feel confusing and hard to deal with. By getting all these thoughts out of our minds and down on paper, it's easier to manage our reactions to climate change information. It's time to write about our emotions, **so grab your climate journal!**

What do I feel?

Hopeless – sometimes, I tend to feel quite hopeless because there is so much to fix, it feels as if progress is slow and we are running out of time. It's also hard to remember that I, as a single individual, can't fix this issue entirely myself.

Scared – I feel scared of the future and what will happen. When people don't care enough, it causes more fear as well. It hurts to see our world having consistent downfalls. I also feel uneasy in my stomach because of butterflies, but not the good kind.

Listening to music and talking to someone I love helps me calm down so that I don't spiral. This helps in many situations because being in isolation causes you to overthink. In addition, it is comforting to read positive news of action that is being taken around the world. It helps to remember that while the world is undergoing many changes, there are many people who are working together to change this.

Aarushi, USA

1. Notice and name it!

Let's name some emotions that we might feel when we think about climate change. What feelings can you name? **Write them down!**

2. Think it!

Some days we will need to accept that climate anxiety is with us. We can do this gently, without judgements, just noticing that we are feeling this. Remember we mentioned 'Mr Climate Anxiety'? This is him.

Now imagine we are on a road trip with Mr Climate Anxiety. Who do we want behind the wheel of our electric car? Do we want Mr Climate Anxiety to drive? NO! We want to drive, obviously! Mr Climate Anxiety is a

TERRIBLE driver. He lives in the Scarcity Zone and likes to drive straight toward all the scariest things because that's what he pays attention to.

Can you remember some thoughts you've had about climate change in the past? Are there some like the ones above, which might be a clue that Mr Climate Anxiety was at the wheel? **Jot them down in your climate journal!**

3. Feel it!

Emotions happen in our minds, but also in our bodies! They can be felt as physical 'sensations' in your body. Sometimes they feel great, like a rush of excitement when you have scored a winning goal, or the 'warm and fuzzies' when you see a kitten.

Other times, these sensations can leave us feeling unsettled or upset. Remember that fight, flight or freeze system? These might feel like nervous butterflies in your stomach, or your heart pumping faster, or even a little dizziness. We might feel a bit panicky. Journal ready? Remind yourself of where in your body you generally hold your worries. Where were you feeling the fight, flight or freeze in your body?

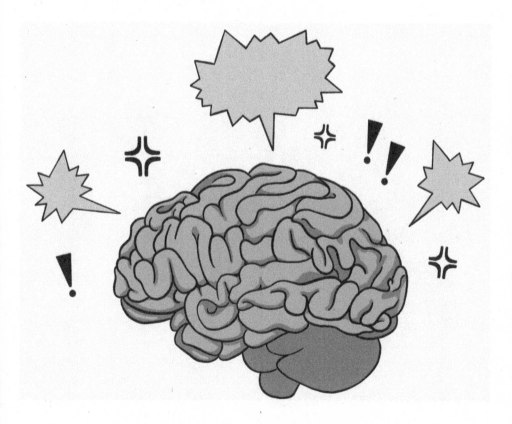

Oh hello, Mr Climate Anxiety... You again...

Remember, we want to be in the driving seat. We don't want our fears steering us. Would we trust them to take us in the direction we would like to go? Sometimes it's helpful to tell Mr Climate Anxiety to move over so that we can take back the wheel and steer ourselves in a more helpful direction!

We can do this by asking ourselves if these scary thoughts or worries are actually true.

Don't believe everything you think

This might seem strange, but just because we think something in one moment doesn't actually mean it's true! It can be hard to remember this when we are feeling worried. Our brain always wants to be right and can forget that it's sometimes wrong. We can think of these thoughts as 'unhelpful'.

Let's challenge some of those unhelpful thoughts!

Can you remember a time you had an unhelpful thought and you believed at the time that it was true? **Try writing down** one of those thoughts that you now know probably isn't true, but at the time you thought it was.

We use an example below that we hear people say quite often, which is, 'Nobody cares about climate change!' This thought is not a fact and is actually quite unhelpful sometimes because it can make us feel sad, lonely and unmotivated to take action.

Once you've written this unhelpful thought down, cross it out, squiggle over it or draw a funny face over it. Then come up with some thoughts that might be more helpful that can help us squash that unhelpful voice. What are some thoughts that help you feel empowered?

We like to do it like this:

How much climate information is too much at once?

It's so important to stay informed, but it's easy to feel overwhelmed if we aren't careful about the WAY we learn climate information. Luckily, there are helpful ways to learn more about the climate crisis and be kind to our mind at the same time! You'll find out how to do this in the next few chapters.

Chapter 6

Climate Stings

Climate stings or triggers can be sounds, noises, thoughts, smells, memories, or any kind of information that causes our brain to react in a startled way. You know when you hear a loud bang, like a firework going off? It makes us feel surprised, and that's our brain saying 'What was that?! What should I do?'

It's important to think about what triggers our eco-emotions. This way we can understand that 'I am feeling angry because I keep seeing people littering' or 'I heard on the radio that there are going to be more floods because of **global warming** and it's raining really hard today. Now I feel a tightness in my throat.'

Once we know what stings, we can name the eco-emotions they cause and pinpoint where they are coming from. We can then remind ourselves that 'This is just how my body and mind react when I hear something sad or scary, and that's okay.'

We aren't saying that you should ignore your emotions or try to avoid these stings! It's okay to not feel okay about what is happening with the planet. But finding your stingers helps to take the power out of these emotions, and gives us some mental space to think about how we want to react. By understanding what bothers you, scares you or makes you angry, you will automatically be more prepared to support yourself when you encounter these stings.

What do you think some of your climate stings or triggers might be?

Equal airtime

Airtime means what plays on the radio or on TV, and for how long. Equal airtime means that for all the negative news and information we hear, we are allowing ourselves to be equally open to positive facts and solutions.

This can be difficult; because news headlines want to grab our attention, they often use really scary headlines so our brains react to them! If that's all that we take in, it's hard to do climate work and feel mentally safe. That's why it's so important to create a balance.

There are lots of amazing resources online that tell the stories of people all over the world who are taking climate action, new technologies to help the planet and positive things happening right now. Asking an adult to help you find these is a great way to feel connected and balanced.

Doomscrolling

Do you have your own phone, tablet or computer? Do you have a TV at your house? If so, you're probably familiar with screen time. Screen time is the time you spend watching or interacting with these digital devices.

During the COVID-19 pandemic, we started to hear the word **DOOMSCROLLING** a lot. This basically means having your eyes glued to a computer or mobile device and soaking up negative, frightening news, which can easily eat up hours of your time. Because lots of us were looking for information about COVID-19, it meant that our brains were focused on a constant stream of scary information (and also a lot of fake information). Unfortunately, the longer we doomscroll, the worse we end up feeling.

Remember, our brains look for danger and don't always know how to process it! The part of our brain that produces the fight, flight or freeze response is evolutionarily older and quite stuck in its ways. It doesn't really understand Instagram or the evening news, so when it sees dangerous information, it's confused, it wants to react...and it wants more! Imagine trying to explain TikTok to your great-grandmother...she'd probably be totally baffled, right?

Here are some top tips to ditch doomscrolling:

- Decide what time of day is best for you to look at social media, read environmental news or learn more about climate change. Pick a time that you usually feel more strong or **RESILIENT** and when you will less likely feel triggered. Avoid doing this first thing in the morning or just before bed, if you've just had a fight with a friend or a family member, or if you're feeling unwell or a bit down in general.

- Limit your time. Set a timer and stick to it! This is hard because social media is designed to keep you scrolling. **Remember, you are the boss! You can step away.** You can also set locks on a lot of devices. It's okay to ask for an adult's help with this. They will probably be really impressed and maybe even take the signal from you to put their own phone down more!

- Actively look for positive stories! Follow activists and groups that inspire you.

- Plan something nice to do after you've been reading climate news. When that timer goes off, do an activity that takes you out of that digital zone and reconnects you with your environment. Go for a walk with a family member, chat with a friend or play with your pet! Find something that calms you down so that those thoughts aren't running circles around your head, telling you to reach for that phone again.

We can allow for both comfortable and uncomfortable feelings to exist. Keep in mind: these exercises aren't meant to make you feel happy about climate change; they're meant to make you feel stronger. By noticing what makes you feel climate anxiety or other strong emotions, you can harness them and make them work for you instead of against you. With this tool, you learn to move from the

Scarcity Zone to the Abundance Zone and put your plans in motion.

Try writing in your climate journal about these topics:

- When was the last time I felt really upset about something bad happening to the planet?
- What did I hear, see or experience just before I felt that anger, fear or sadness?
- What did I do when this happened?
- What could I do in the future when this happens?
- What do I want to do about this? How can I use this strong feeling as motivation for an action that will help me and the planet? (This is a great time to get a grown-up involved to help you make plans.)

Chapter 7

Let's Flip It

We aren't saying 'Be happy about climate change!' Not at all! But it's important to remember that we all have a range of emotions that come and go (a bit like clouds in the sky, or leaves floating down a stream). If we don't give equal airtime or attention to the positive, then we risk feeling taken over by the strong, less enjoyable emotions. That can leave us feeling helpless, and stop us from feeling able to take climate action.

Luckily, there are already so many brilliant and creative people working to reverse climate change. Because of the actions of all these people, we are seeing climate successes all around the world.

For example, did you know that:

- In the USA, the population of bald eagles (which was once on the brink of extinction) is now four times higher than it was when conservation efforts began![1]
- In 1985, scientists discovered a hole in the ozone layer (a protective 'shield' of gases in the Earth's stratosphere that protects us from the sun's

radiation). This hole was caused by us, humans. However, thanks to people realizing the problem and changing their behaviour, and governments changing their policies banning the use of certain chemicals, our ozone layer is now on track to be completely healed over in the next 30 years.[2]

- The Fridays For Future movement has inspired over 16 million young people (and their adult allies!) to go out and strike to raise awareness of the climate emergency, in over 216 countries (and 8500 cities) around the world – and counting![3]

- 'Plogging' is a new fitness craze that started with runners getting fed up by the litter that they saw. So now, as they jog, they pick up rubbish! Plogging is catching on all over the world.

- A Nairobi, Kenya-based engineer is transforming plastic waste into bricks that are seven times stronger than regular bricks, helping to build homes in the community.[4]

- In Pakistan, the 10 Billion Tree Tsunami programme is restoring over 350,000 hectares (over 1300 square miles) of forest. But even better, the programme is offering work to over 60,000 people who lost their jobs or were unable to work during the COVID-19 pandemic.[5]

With all that amazing climate news in mind, think for a moment about all the possibilities! Think about the images you've seen of new areas being rewilded (meaning, 'returned to nature') or the amazing technology that is pulling pollution out of the air and plastic out of the sea. Think of all the protesters filling the streets, demanding climate action. You are one of millions of climate warriors who care. And we have the technology we need already!

I have a friend on every continent fighting for the same thing. How can we lose? It's almost mind-blowing. There are people in every country working to stop global warming; that is inspiring.

Mitzi Jonelle Tan, youth activist, organizer
for Fridays For Future, Philippines

Now let's try another experiment...

1. Notice it!

After reading all these awesome facts about climate solutions and positive change, do you have a bit of hope? Do you feel a glimmer of light and inspiration? Do you notice any change in how you feel?

2. Name it!

Let's look for some ENJOYABLE emotions that we might feel when we think about climate change.

Do you feel any of these emotions when you hear positive stories of climate change, or when you think about your own climate work? How about amazing new projects and technologies? Are there any other positive emotions you can name? You guessed it: **write these down in your climate journal!**

3. Think it!

There are so many people doing so much good work to help the planet!

This is possible!

We are unstoppable!

Can you remember some positive thoughts you've had when you think about climate change? **Jot them down. Don't cross out these thoughts, though!** Instead of challenging these thoughts, like we did in Chapter 6, let's help them grow stronger instead. Why not think thoughts that help you feel empowered?

How about something like this:

4. Feel it!

Where in our bodies do we feel these enjoyable emotions? You might still feel the butterflies, or it might feel like one of those warm, fuzzy feelings you get when you have a nice hug. Do you feel more planted in your chair or on your feet? Can you look around you or remember three beautiful things you've seen in nature? **Write these down.** You might want to put your hand on your heart and connect with that feeling of optimism and strength. Take a deep breath and thank your emotions for giving you signals about your feelings, your environment and what is important to you.

Chapter 8

Self-Care Is Your Secret Weapon!

Practising self-care means looking after yourself and doing things that you know are good for your mind and body so that you can complete your goals in a healthy way.

At the beginning of an aeroplane trip, the flight attendant will tell you that if there is an emergency, you must put on your own oxygen mask first before helping anyone else. After all, how can you help others if you can't breathe yourself? The same goes for climate work; we need to take care of ourselves in order to help this wonderful world.

Also, the flight attendant will instruct adults to help younger people with their masks, so this means that you can ask adults to help when you need it. This is another helpful message – it's okay to get the help you need from your trusted adults to become a self-care champion.

'But how can I think about myself when the ice caps are melting?'

Imagine it's the night before a big running race. Would we say 'Okay, after all the work I've put in, I think I'll eat a cheeseburger and go to bed really late'? Of course not! We want to give it our best shot, rest and nourish ourselves, and gear ourselves up for success. If runners are willing to do that for their sport, we think your efforts toward saving the planet deserve AT LEAST that same level of self-care!

How do I practise self-care?

Although everyone has different methods of self-care, there are certain tricks that lots of awesome climate warriors have told us they benefit from:

- **Connect with others.** By speaking with friends and family about how we feel, what we want to do and how we want to do it, we don't feel like solving global warming is all on our shoulders. We can feel motivated, inspired and accepted when we connect with others.
- **Pay attention to scarcity versus abundance.** By doing this, we can turn up the volume on our self-care if we're in the Scarcity Zone, or feel encouraged to keep going if we're thriving in the Abundance Zone.
- **Take breaks from climate work.** It's really important to allow ourselves to 'switch off' sometimes. This means switching off from both climate information and climate work. We have to remind ourselves that rest is essential in letting our brains reset a bit. With little breaks here and there, we can come back to our climate work with fresh energy and more creative ideas.

- **Interact with nature.** This is one of our favourites! What better way to care for ourselves than by enjoying what we're trying to protect? Many people have disconnected with nature, and some even think of nature as ours to take something away from. This is a huge problem, and it's our job to shift this mindset. We wouldn't pollute our homes, our rooms, or our friends' houses, so how can we make such a mess of our beautiful planet? Sure, if you're reading this, you probably aren't somebody who takes nature for granted. Still, it can be easy to forget to unplug from day-to-day life and plug back into nature. More on this subject later!

- **Have a balanced schedule.** Although we want everyone doing lots of amazing climate work, it's important to create a balance with other activities so that we don't run out of energy. Deciding specifically when and for how long we are going to do our climate activities will help us manage our time.

- **Celebrate successes.** It's important to acknowledge our accomplishments. This helps us look forward to our next goal or challenge. Our brains love a treat!

My mum has helped me think and talk about my climate emotions. Mum is really encouraging. She comes to the marches with us. We all dressed up in scuba gear for a protest to raise awareness about rising seas. We can talk to her if we are upset. After a protest we went with new friends for pizza.

Ben, UK

Grab your climate journal again...
it's time for a feel-good exercise!

- What are some of the things in your life that seem to instantly make you feel good?
- What helps when you are feeling stressed, upset or overwhelmed?
- What makes you feel like your best self?

Self-care plans are different for everyone, so try out different things. Be flexible and figure out what works for YOU! Do a few of these activities each day...and remember – you can always dial up the self-care if you are feeling worried or a bit wobbly.

Connecting with our planet

People all around the world have so many incredible ways of connecting with nature, and there are loads of words, in many languages, to describe it. For example, in Germany, *Waldeinsamkeit* means 'wandering alone in the woods', and in Aboriginal communities in Australia, *dadirri* means 'deeply listening' to nature.

I think connecting with nature helps me a lot. When I moved back to London I had to experience nature in a different way than when I lived in the countryside. Because we are in an urban environment and it's not the same. I took up foraging. I'd go around the streets of London and look for wild fruit, mushrooms, all sorts. Sometimes it's just acknowledging the beauty of things, just being able to identify different trees and flowers and it's amazing how this alleviates climate anxiety.

Daze, youth climate activist, UK

You don't have to actually be in nature to connect with it. Although most of us would rather feel sand between our toes at the beach or the frosty morning air of a walk through the forest, we can also use some visualizations to reconnect with the natural world. This can really help us if we are stuck inside and feeling overwhelmed by bad news about the planet.

Let's return to nature. Sort of...

Remember a time that you were outside and felt really connected to all the natural beauty. Where were you? At the beach? In a forest? At the park? What were you doing? Were you by yourself or with others?

Close your eyes as you remember. Try to take a mental photograph of this moment. Try to focus on one thing in that picture. It may be a tree, sand, water or whatever else. Take some deep breaths and give the beauty and calmness of that object your full attention. What are three little things you notice about how you feel, what you observe? Can you remember any smells or noises? Just allow yourself to be in this moment briefly.

See? We can experience a connection to the natural world any time. You can return to this picture in your mind whenever you need a little dose of nature. Meditating, or looking at pictures of nature, can also help with this.

Just one more reminder: be gentle with yourself. Try to speak to yourself the same way that you would speak to a friend who is having big feelings about something important to them. You'd probably use a kind and encouraging voice, right? Try to use this voice with yourself as you start down this long road!

How do I cope when things don't go as I plan? I have an amazing friend who gave the best advice. 'Don't think about the outcome. Just do what feels right.' This takes off the weight of feeling like you have to accomplish something. What you may see as a failure may just be one of the stepping stones to what you are meant to do. Keep going.

Daze, youth climate activist, UK

Chapter 9

Your Place in the Hive

We all have our role to play. Think about your favourite stories – either in books, movies or TV shows. No one character does everything on their own. They all have at least one companion, guide or sidekick. Each character in the battle for our planet has their own distinct act to play. You're not THE ONLY hero in this story, because in order for us to defeat the climate change villain, we need MILLIONS of heroes. This is good news, because it means you don't have to save the world alone! You are here to HELP save the world. This is not all on you!

Since it will take everyone to pitch in and fight this issue, I'd have my role be instilling an emotion in others where they truly care about Planet Earth and are proactive to take action, no matter how big or small. This way, we could all be heroes in saving the world.

Aarushi, USA

Your climate story

Writing your own climate story will help you understand what role you want to play. To do this, ask yourself some big questions! We already know that climate change is the sneaky villain, but what characters do we need to battle it? Which one will you be?

Are you the activist, the tree planter, the community builder, the organizer, the loudspeaker, the rebel, the policy changer, the techie, the guardian, the justice seeker?

Where's that climate journal?

Okay, ready? It's time to write out your climate story!

- What are some things you care about? (Animals? Friends? Family? Nature? Equality?)
- What makes you feel big, unpleasant emotions about climate change? (Pollution? Endangered species? Injustice?)
- Who made you care about climate change? (A teacher? An activist? Just loving nature?)
- How would a friend describe you? (All the fabulous things about you!)
- Where would you like to grow stronger? What are some small steps you can take to improve in this area?
- What are your strengths? (List them all, from football to kindness.)
- Who do you want your character to be in your climate story? (Think big and small!)
- How can you use your strengths to do good climate work? (Get creative with this. Do you make friends easily? Form an eco-club. Are you a great writer? Write about the climate and show it to the world!)

Everyone has an amazing and unique skill set and we can all work together to practise climate action.

Daze, youth climate activist, UK

Chapter 10

Climate Actions (Buzzing Towards Success)

> At my school I run a club where we try to help our teachers include climate justice and climate emotions in their lessons. I also volunteer at Force of Nature and Create the Future, and sometimes with Sierra Club. I feel alive when I take action – I feel happy, purposeful, determined and fulfilled.
>
> Tupelo, climate justice activist, USA

Now that you've thought about what you care about and what role you want to play, it's time to think about your climate action goals.

Need more inspiration? The world is full of examples of young people absolutely going for it. For example, have you heard of Mari Copeny? When she was eight years old, she wrote a letter to President Barack Obama (who was president of the United States at the time), alerting him to the poisoned water system in her town. Obama visited the city and pledged $100 million to help fix the water problem. Mari (aka 'Little Miss Flint') shows what can happen when we communicate with our politicians. She is even planning on running for president of the United States when she'll be old enough! I think she'd have our vote.

Or how about Haaziq Kazi, from Pune, India? Haaziq is super-passionate about ocean conservation. When he was only 11 years old he designed a ship called ERVIS that cleans up lots of plastic from the ocean. He also set up the ERVIS Foundation, to educate and inspire us all to use less plastic.

Amazing, right? A single act and commitment to the planet has made such a difference.

Feeling inspired? We hope so, because now it's time to set goals of your own!

We always want our goals to be challenging, but achievable. 'Save the planet on Wednesday before football practice' is not a good goal because it's impossible to achieve; if someone were able to do this they would have done it already! It's important for us to set specific, realistic goals instead.

Climate action plans in flight!

Let's use some imaginary climate activists...

James and Marie are brother and sister. James is 14 and Marie is 15. Ever since they were little they have loved rockpooling (sometimes called 'tide pooling'), building sand castles and swimming in the sea near their home. Lately, they have been really worried about all the plastic they see at the beach. They already do litter-picks, but they want to do more. Their friend tells them about a conservation programme called the World Wildlife Fund (WWF) and all the good work they are doing. James and Marie want to support this programme...but how?

Their teacher tells them about a 5k race happening in their town next month, and James and Marie have a great idea! They both love sports, so why not sign up for the race and raise money for the WWF at the same time?

Boom, they have their BIG GOAL: run the 5k and raise money for the WWF.

Now that James and Marie have their big goal, it's time to get specific. How will they prepare for the race and raise money for this cause? Here's what they come up with:

- They ask their parents to help sign them up for the 5k.
- They begin training together three days a week, getting enough rest, and eating well.
- Leading up to the race, they each ask 10 people a week to donate money.
- They ask their friends to join them in the race, or just to come and cheer them on so more and more people are supporting climate action.
- Finally, they decide to celebrate their hard work by having a picnic with their friends on the beach after the race!

Your turn!

What big goal could you set for the end of the month? Don't be shy – **write it in your climate journal!** Now let's break your goal down into smaller bits:

- What steps do you need to take to make this big goal happen?
- What could you do TODAY to get started? This is your goal for today.
- Who could you talk to about this goal and/or who could help you achieve this goal? A friend? A teacher? Another adult? We all need help, so don't be afraid to reach out.
- What are you going to do to celebrate when you achieve this goal? Be sure to write this down so you will stay motivated to stick to your plans!

Need ideas? Why not...

- Start an eco-club at school.
- Get 10 people to switch to green energy in the next two months.
- Ask your family to go meat-free during the week.
- Write a letter to your MP or local councillor about some steps they can take to influence people's behaviour.
- Get your friends to join you on a weekly litter-pick.
- Get your family to compost.
- Buy no new clothes or toys for a month.

- Have a conversation about climate change with a new person every day for a week.
- Tell others what actions they can take.
- Talk to your headteacher about changes the school could make (like switching to green energy, reducing plastic use, cutting down on waste).
- Go to a protest (and get friends and family to come along).

Chapter 11

Buzzkills

> Even though I may get upset I take a step back to think about what may have gone wrong and realize that setbacks are bound to happen. I plan out what I'm going to do next, and if I need help, I ask people around me because sometimes other people have great ideas that may make what I'm working on so much better.
>
> Aarushi, USA

Perfect doesn't get anything done!

Listen, folks: we all have disappointments, and we all have setbacks. Sometimes we make plans and things around us change. Sometimes this is in our control, and sometimes it's not.

Maybe we're trying to eat less meat, but we go to a birthday party where they're only serving chicken nuggets.

Guess what: it's okay to be kind to ourselves in a difficult moment like this! Maybe we set big goals for our climate work and then get overwhelmed or make mistakes...that's okay, too! We don't always get everything right. That's why it's so important to remind ourselves that the climate change battle is a marathon, not a sprint. There will be lots of problems and challenges along the way, and all we can do is take the next best step with the information that we have.

As long as you are trying your best, you aren't failing.

Sometimes, despite our best efforts, an action we try to take to help the planet doesn't quite work. This can happen for lots of reasons, especially if there are other people involved, because we can't decide what other people think or do. When this happens, we call it a 'setback'. Here's what to do if a setback comes along.

Quick tricks to snap back from setbacks

S: **Seek** support. Who can I talk to when I feel disappointed or worried or overwhelmed? Who will understand? Who will encourage me?

E: **Evaluate** the setback. What didn't work and why? Can it still work? If so, how can you move forward?

T: **Take** on an easy task. If you have just suffered a big setback or felt a big emotion, hit reset by doing a few simple tasks that support the planet. Do a litter-pick, sign some online petitions, call a friend and make some climate action plans.

B: **Believe** that you can overcome setbacks and move forward. Remind yourself of all the positive things you have accomplished – climate-related or not!

A: **Acknowledge** the right amount of responsibility. Did you show up for yourself? Did you do your best? This also means not beating yourself up if the setback was beyond your control.

C: **Compartmentalize** – put it into separate boxes or 'compartments'. Setbacks are a normal part of life, and this doesn't mean that you have to go back to the very beginning. Remember, one setback does not delete all the other positive actions you have achieved!

K: **Keep** moving forward!

Making plans ahead of time will help you navigate when things don't go as planned.

In your journal, follow this model to write up your ideas for SETBACKS:

S: Seek support. . . . .

. . . .

E: Evaluate the setback. . . . .

. . . .

T: Take on an easy task. . . . .

. . . .

B: Believe. . . . .

. . . .

A: Acknowledge. . . . .

. . . .

C: Compartmentalize. . . . .

. . . .

K: Keep moving forward! . . . .

. . . .

There you go. Now you can SNAP BACK FROM
SETBACKS!

Chapter 12

Be Unstoppable!

I want to say to other young activists, or those just starting their climate work, that I'm very proud of you for taking a step to learn about this issue and taking action. It is truly incredible to see more youth stand their ground. The world is a big place, but together we can solve this issue. Never give up!

Aarushi, USA

Congratulations, eco-warrior! You now understand:

- how the climate crisis can affect your mental health
- how to notice and name your emotions
- how to release unhelpful emotions if they become too strong
- how important self-care is
- the role that you want to play in the fight against climate change.

And you're now equipped with:

- the tools to communicate with others
- a plan for your climate action work
- ways to celebrate when you complete your goals.

You can come back to this book any time you need to, and don't forget about your climate journal once you're finished reading! Thank yourself and be proud of all the work you have done here. You've taken the time to care for your mental health so that you can help save the planet. You've got the tools to stay strong and resilient. We may be at the end of this book, but you're only at the beginning of your eco-journey.

Always remember:

- Be kind to yourself.
- Believe in yourself and your endless power.
- You are unstoppable!

Buzzwords (Glossary)

Here are a few helpful phrases or words that you will have seen in this book, usually in bold text.

Abundance The opposite of scarcity. Abundance allows us to feel that we have and are enough! In the Abundance Zone we feel that our actions are important, that we can make a difference and that we can influence other people. We feel resilient and powerful.

Allies People who are on our team. They often believe in the same causes and are in a good position to help us achieve our aims. We can also be allies for others.

Anxiety Our anxiety is like an inner alarm. It says, 'Something is wrong!' This is an awesome superpower that has helped our ancestors survive danger for thousands of years. Sometimes this alarm helps you, like if a car is speeding towards you or someone makes you uncomfortable! We can thank our anxiety for the times it protects us...but sometimes, we need to hit mute when it isn't helping us.

Asset Something that is valuable or useful, something that people want or that they can use to get something they want.

Climate action The things we do to help the planet. Climate actions both big and small matter. Climate action is our secret weapon against climate change, and also against negative eco-emotions. When we see our positive work, we begin to feel stronger and more powerful.

Climate anxiety (also called eco-anxiety) Refers to the distress we experience when we think about, learn about, or hear about, the climate crisis. Although it involves anxiety, it can also include other emotions like anger, guilt and hopelessness. Anybody can experience climate anxiety, and it is not always a bad thing (it shows we care, and it can inspire us to take action). However, sometimes it can feel overwhelming and affect our sleep and ability to concentrate and enjoy life. That's when it becomes important to get support.

Climate change or **global warming** The warming of our planet. More and more problems are popping up because of human behaviour, and they'll just get worse if we don't adjust our habits. These problems include melting glaciers, stronger storms, the extinction of species, damage to the oceans and ecosystems, drought, wildfires and more.

Climate justice The climate crisis is not just about defending the environment, but also fighting for the rights of all the people around the world who are treated unfairly (often when they are trying to take important climate action).

Climate psychology Understanding how our minds react when we think about, hear information about or experience climate change. There are a few different areas of climate psychology. One is the **direct impacts** of climate change. This is how people feel and act after they have experienced climate change. This could happen after a flood or wildfire, for example. People may feel trauma, loss or grief.

Climate psychologists also study the **indirect impacts** of climate change. This relates to future concerns about how the climate will change. We might feel anxious, worried, angry or unsure about the safety of the planet or ourselves.

Climate psychologists also study how we communicate about climate change. This is important, because how we talk about climate change can make a huge difference in how people respond to the information they have at hand. **If we are clever in how we communicate about climate change**, we can help others understand the importance of climate action and help them feel that their view matters.

Doomscrolling Having your eyes glued to a computer or mobile phone and soaking up negative, frightening news, which can easily eat up hours of your time.

Eco-emotions Any emotional response your body has to hearing climate change information. There are so many emotions you might feel, and they're all normal. In fact, you can use any of these feelings as motivation in your fight against climate change!

Global South This refers to a large number of countries in areas like Asia, Latin America, Oceania and Africa that have been historically colonized. Because of this, they have been economically and socially **marginalized** and are not as well developed as countries in the Global North (for example, in North America and Europe).

Greenwashing When groups (usually businesses or governments) try to convince everybody that they are taking action to help the planet, when, in fact, they are not.

Marginalized Being made deliberately less powerful or influential.

Psychology Studying and learning more about the human mind and how it changes our behaviour, our thoughts and our actions. Part of our psychology is hard-wired into us at birth, and some we learn from life experiences.

Resilient Getting back up when you get knocked down!

Scarcity Not having enough. When we are thinking about our climate work from the Scarcity Zone, it can be really hard for us to see all the good we're doing. We think thoughts like 'Whatever I do won't matter' or 'I haven't done well enough'.

Social injustices Ways in which people from different communities or backgrounds are treated unfairly, or they have access to fewer opportunities in life.

Symbiosis A relationship that is cooperative, where two (or more) different things get along together and help each other out.

Trigger A smell, noise or any kind of information that startles the brain. When we know what our triggers are, we can name the emotions they cause. This helps to take the power out of strong, unpleasant emotions. We can also help ourselves by taking note of what triggers our positive emotions!

For Adults and Educators (How to Support Your Eco-Warriors)

Adults, could we have a moment? Firstly, your children are amazing for their interest and commitment to the planet, which is probably a testament to you. Well done for cultivating modern climate warriors. While we want to empower our children as well as ourselves, and while we know that climate anxiety can be relieved by climate action, we want to instil the narrative that though our individual work is essential, this is not the responsibility of the individual. We are part of a broken system that has, in a calculated way, led us to this point. As parents or guardians, we implore you to support the action your children want to take and to do this by being an ally. You are in a position of power. Learn as much as you can and talk about climate change.

Actions you can take:

1. Talk about climate change.
2. Switch to a more vegetable-based diet.
3. Switch to a renewable energy supplier.

4. Make your home more energy efficient.
5. Use cars less.
6. Stop flying.
7. Divest your pension from fossil fuels.
8. Divest your investments from fossil fuels.
9. Refuse or reject excessive consumption.
10. Reduce what you use.
11. Reuse as much as you can.
12. Recycle as much as you can.
13. Use your consumer choice.
14. Protest.
15. Vote.[1]

Understand what your child or student already knows about climate change

It's best to begin by figuring out what your child or student already knows. Ask open questions:

- What have you heard about global warming or climate change?
- Who talks to you about this?
- How do you feel about this happening?
- How do your friends feel about climate change?
- Is anyone doing anything about it?
- What could we, as a family (or school or community), be doing about it?

Key tips for climate conversations

- Ensure that you're in an emotionally safe space yourself. If you're currently feeling climate anxiety, it's not the best time to kick off this topic with a child. For some ideas and support for yourself, you can find more information in our book, *Turn the Tide on Climate Anxiety: Sustainable Action for Your Mental Health and the Planet* (which is designed for adult readers).

- It is important that you feel confident in your knowledge of climate change and its impact (we recommend Mark Maslin's *How to Save Our Planet: The Facts*), but remember that you don't have to be a climate scientist to talk about climate change. If you don't know the answer to a question, just be honest! Do some research and revisit the topic later.

- Keep the conversation short, simple and age-appropriate.

- Don't over-explain; if you feel yourself ranting or monologuing, take a breath. This is a great way to demonstrate 'thinking before you speak' to your children.

- Give your children space to think and express themselves.

- Be completely focused and set aside time for follow-up conversations and questions.

- Talk about how you feel, but be careful not to project your eco-emotions onto your children.

- Commit to specific actions and decide how you will celebrate your successes.

- Thank yourself for showing up. Bookend these talks with nice activities (go for a walk, make a meal, plant some seeds, donate or do a litter-pick).

We helped to develop some resources in the UK to support adults to talk with young people about climate change. They were coproduced by the Educational & Child Psychologists Westminster Team and Kensington & Chelsea Educational Psychology Consultation Service. They can be accessed for free, via our website (www.climatepsychologists.com/resources).

About the Authors

Megan Kennedy-Woodard and Dr Patrick Kennedy-Williams are founders of Climate Psychologists and authors of *Turn the Tide on Climate Anxiety: Sustainable Action for Your Mental Health and the Planet*. They are also the creators of www.MindandPlanet.com, a platform that serves both educators and business leaders to nurture the climate-empowered leaders of tomorrow.

Megan and Patrick share two wild and wonderful children, who inspire them each and every day. Their home is an ever-growing zoo (despite Patrick's initial protests). As a family they can usually be found outdoors.

About the Illustrator

Jordanna George is an illustrator and comic artist from the T'Sou-ke Nation on the west coast of Canada. They earned a degree in visual art from the University of Victoria, and now live in Burnaby, BC on the unceded lands of the Musqueam, Squamish, Tsleil-Waututh and Kwikwetlem nations. They love fantasy and science fiction, as well as exploring themes of identity, belonging and hope, especially pertaining to LGBTQ+ and Indigenous narratives. When they aren't drawing, they enjoy reading, gaming and playing with the nearest fluffy animal.

Endnotes

Chapter 1

1   Natural England (2021) *The Children's People and Nature Survey for England: Summer Holidays 2021*, which you can read at www.gov.uk/government/statistics/the-childrens-people-and-nature-survey-for-england-summer-holidays-2021-official-statistics/the-childrens-people-and-nature-survey-for-england-summer-holidays-2021-official-statistics

2   According to Office for National Statistics (ONS) data: www.ons.gov.uk/peoplepopulationandcommunity/populationandmigration/populationestimates/bulletins/annualmidyearpopulationestimates/mid2020

3   Okay maybe we are being a little hard on mosquitos, they do pollinate and provide food for other animals... But still, OUCH!

4   More facts about bees can be found at the Science Learning Hub (2007) 'Bees – fun facts.' 30 June, which you can read at www.sciencelearn.org.nz/resources/2002-bees-fun-facts and also World Wildlife Fund (no date) 'Top 10 facts about bees', at www.wwf.org.uk/learn/fascinating-facts/bees

Chapter 2

1   Mark Maslin (2014) *Climate Change: A Very Short Introduction.* Oxford: Oxford University Press.

2   Mark Maslin (2021) *How to Save Our Planet: The Facts.* London: Penguin Random House.

3   Al Gore said this in an interview with *National Geographic* magazine in 2017. You can also check it out online by going to www.nationalgeographic.com/magazine/article/3-questions-al-gore-climate-change

4   For more information about MAPA and what we can all do to amplify their voices, visit https://fridaysforfuture.org/newsletter/edition-no-1-what-is-mapa-and-why-should-we-pay-attention-to-it

Chapter 7

1   The return of bald eagles in the USA is being described as one of the most successful conservation attempts in history. There are lots of reports about this, including in *The New York Times*: www.nytimes.com/2021/03/25/climate/how-many-bald-eagles-united-states.html

2   The repair of the hole in the ozone layer is a great example of people, scientists and governments coming together to solve an environmental problem. For a great explanation of this, see https://earthobservatory.nasa.gov/blogs/eokids/wp-content/uploads/sites/6/2020/05/26_Ozone_6_2020_508.pdf

3   The Fridays For Future movement keeps growing and growing! Find out the latest statistics about the strikes at https://fridaysforfuture.org/what-we-do/strike-statistics

4   The inventor's company is called Gjenge Makers, and her incredible story can be found at www.africanews. com/2020/12/08/nairobi-based-company-turns-plastic-waste-into-eco-friendly-bricks

5   To learn more about the 10 Billion Tree Tsunami programme, visit www.aljazeera.com/news/2020/4/29/pakistans-virus-idled-workers-hired-to-plant-trees

For Adults and Educators

1   Mark Maslin (2021) *How to Save Our Planet: The Facts.* London: Penguin Random House.